NEW JERSEY

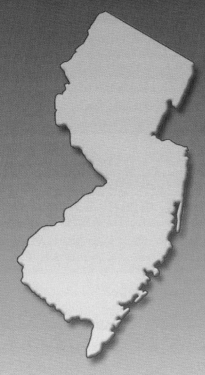

by Ann Malaspina

GARETH**STEVENS**

PUBLISHING

A Member of the WRC Media Family of Companies

Please visit our web site at: www.garethstevens.com
For a free color catalog describing Gareth Stevens Publishing's
list of high-quality books and multimedia programs, call
1-800-542-2595 (USA) or 1-800-387-3178 (Canada).
Gareth Stevens Publishing's fax: (414) 332-3567.

Library of Congress Cataloging-in-Publication Data

Malaspina, Ann, 1957-
     New Jersey / Ann Malaspina.
         p. cm. — (Portraits of the states)
     Includes bibliographical references and index.
     ISBN 0-8368-4629-X (lib. bdg.)
     ISBN 0-8368-4648-6 (softcover)
     1. New Jersey—Juvenile literature. I. Title. II. Series.
     F134.3.M35   2005
     974.9—dc22   2005042631

This edition first published in 2006 by
Gareth Stevens Publishing
A Member of the WRC Media Family of Companies
330 West Olive Street, Suite 100
Milwaukee, WI 53212 USA

This edition copyright © 2006 by Gareth Stevens, Inc.

Editorial direction: Mark J. Sachner
Project manager: Jonatha A. Brown
Editor: Betsy Rasmussen
Art direction and design: Tammy West
Picture research: Diane Laska-Swanke
Indexer: Walter Kronenberg
Production: Jessica Morris and Robert Kraus

Picture credits: Cover, Atlantic City Convention & Visitors Authority; pp. 4, 17,
24, 26, 28 © Gibson Stock Photography; pp. 5, 7, 8 © Corel; p. 9 © Mansell/
Time & Life Pictures/Getty Images; pp. 10, 11 © Library of Congress; p. 15
© Painet; p. 21 © Carol Kitman; p. 22 © Chris Hondros/Getty Images; p. 25
© Stock Montage/Getty Images; p. 27 © Doug Pensinger/Getty Images; p. 29
© Robin Platzer/Time & Life Pictures/Getty Images

Printed in the United States of America

1 2 3 4 5 6 7 8 9 09 08 07 06 05

CONTENTS

Words that are defined in the Glossary appear
in **bold** the first time they are used in the text.

On the Cover: Atlantic City spreads out along the New Jersey shore.

Introduction

New Jersey is a small state with big ideas. The light bulb was **invented** there. The first movies were made there.

The people of New Jersey make goods that are sold near and far. Ships carry tools and machines from the ports of Newark and Elizabeth. Trucks haul canned food over highways. **Cargo** planes fly out of the Newark airport. They carry goods, too.

This state has something for everyone! It has white sandy beaches and big cities. It has quiet forests and busy factories. It has blueberry fields and office buildings. Every day can be exciting in New Jersey.

People of all ages stroll beside the beach at Seaside Heights, New Jersey.

The state flag of New Jersey.

NEW JERSEY FACTS

- Became the 3rd State: December 18, 1787
- Population (2004): 8,698,879
- Capital: Trenton
- Biggest Cities: Newark, Jersey City, Paterson, Elizabeth
- Size: 7,787 square miles (20,168 square kilometers)
- Nickname: The Garden State
- State Tree: Red oak
- State Flower: Purple violet
- State Animal: Horse
- State Bird: Eastern goldfinch

History

Long ago, Native Americans lived in New Jersey. They were the Lenni-Lenape. Their name means "True People." The Lenni-Lenape lived along the Delaware River. They planted corn, beans, and squash. They fished in the rivers and hunted deer in the woods.

European Explorers

In 1524, an Italian explorer sailed up the coast of New Jersey. His name was Giovanni da Verrazano. He was the first white man to explore the area.

In 1609, Henry Hudson sailed up the Hudson River. He was English, but he sailed for the Dutch. The Dutch claimed for themselves the land along the river. They called it New Netherland.

Dutch settlers moved to New Jersey in 1624. Soon, people from Sweden and Finland joined them. The settlers built farms and villages along the Hudson River. Their first town was Bergen.

FUN FACTS

Lenni-Lenape Game

The Lenni-Lenape played a game called Pahsahëman. It was played with a ball. Men played against women. Men kicked the ball, and women threw it. Each team tried to get the ball past the goal posts at one end of the field.

Settlers and Lenni-Lenape

The Europeans called the Lenni-Lenape the Delaware. Europeans traded with them — beads and cloth for beaver furs. Later, the settlers wanted the land. They forced the Lenni-Lenape to move far to the west.

New Jersey Colony

In 1664, the British took New Jersey from the Dutch. By 1702, the area had become a British **colony**. It was one of thirteen colonies in America that were held by Britain.

By the 1770s, many colonists wanted to be free from Great Britain. The king had made them pay heavy taxes. They did not think the taxes were fair. When the king put a tax on tea, they dumped the tea into the sea. The Revolutionary War

Native Americans and settlers from Europe all wanted to live near the beautiful Delaware River.

FUN FACTS

How the State Got Its Name

When the British took New Jersey from the Dutch, they gave it a new name. They named it for the island of Jersey off the coast of Britain.

In colonial times, settlers set up small farms like the one shown in this painting from the mid-1800s.

began the next year, in 1775. The colonies fought for their freedom. Many battles were fought in New Jersey.

The British lost the war in 1783, and the colonies were free. Soon, the leaders of the colonies met. They wrote down new laws for a new country. The leaders of New Jersey played an important part in those meetings. They came up with the idea of a

General George Washington crossed the Delaware River to fight the British during the Revolutionary War.

The 1800s were a time of great change for New Jersey. Roads and railroads were built. Artificial rivers, or

Senate in which each state had the same number of representatives. Four years later, New Jersey became the third state to join the United States. For a few months, the U.S. capital was in Princeton. It was then moved to Trenton, but it did not stay there either.

IN NEW JERSEY'S HISTORY

The Battle of Trenton

The Battle of Trenton took place in 1776. On Christmas night, General George Washington crossed the Delaware River in a boat. The river was full of ice, and a storm blew wind and snow. His soldiers were wet and cold. They hiked 9 miles (14 km) to Trenton and surprised the enemy there. Washington and his men won the battle on December 26.

FACTS

The First Locomotive

In 1825, the first locomotive in the country was made in Hoboken. Its engine was powered by steam.

canals, were dug, too. By the middle of the century, people and goods could easily be moved from place to place.

Locomotives and Silk

At about this time, machines began to take over work that had once been done by hand. Soon, factories sprang up in cities like Paterson and Newark. They made shoes, coaches, steam **locomotives**, and silk. The roads, canals,

and railroads carried these goods north and south. New Jersey was now a center for **industry**.

The Civil War

Trouble began in the middle of the 1800s. Many people in Southern states kept black people as slaves. People in Northern states such as New Jersey did not. Many people wanted to ban slavery all over the country. Yet the slave owners in the South were determined to keep their slaves. Those states decided to form their own

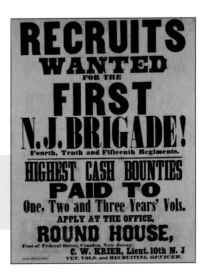

This poster promised money to New Jersey men who would fight in the Civil War.

country, the Confederate States of America.

The two sides started the Civil War in 1861. No battles were fought in New Jersey, but about eighty-eight thousand men from the state joined the battle. They fought for the North. When the North won in 1865, the country united again, and the slaves were set free.

Thomas Edison worked long hours in his workshop to develop his many inventions.

Famous People of New Jersey

Thomas Alva Edison

Born: February 11, 1847, Milan, Ohio

Died: October 18, 1931, West Orange

Thomas Edison was a great inventor who spent most of his life in New Jersey. He was the first person to create an electric light that was safe and useful. He was the first to make a motion picture camera and movies, too. Over the years, Edison invented hundreds of machines and machine parts. Some of his inventions changed the way we live.

Growing Fast

After the war, New Jersey grew. African Americans came up from the South. People from Italy and Ireland came over the ocean, too. Still more people came from other parts of Europe. Most of these newcomers worked in factories. New factories opened, and old ones grew larger. New Jersey was doing very well.

Life changed in the 1930s. The **Great Depression** hit the whole country hard. Prices fell, people lost their jobs, and factories closed. This was a very difficult time for the people of New Jersey. It was years before the state recovered.

Business improved in the 1940s. The country fought in World War II, and New Jersey factories made supplies. After the war, business was good at first. Then, companies started to leave the cities for the outlying areas. Cities lost jobs, good schools, and housing. By this time, factories had polluted the water, soil, and air.

Race riots broke out in Newark in 1967. Twenty-six people were killed.

New Jersey is working to solve its problems. It is ready to meet its challenges.

IN NEW JERSEY'S HISTORY

The Day the Towers Fell

On September 11, 2001, **terrorists** crashed two planes into the World Trade Center in New York City. The "twin towers" fell. Thousands of people died. Hundreds were from New Jersey. Many people who were in New Jersey that day could see the scene from across the river. There was nothing they could do to help.

1524	Giovanni da Verrazano reaches the New Jersey shore.
1609	Henry Hudson sails up the Hudson River.
1624	Dutch settlers move to New Jersey.
1660	Bergen, the first town in New Jersey, is founded.
1664	The British take New Jersey from the Dutch.
1775–1783	New Jersey colonists fight in the Revolutionary War.
1787	New Jersey becomes the third state to join the United States.
1861–1865	New Jersey men fight on the side of the North in the Civil War.
1929–1939	Many people in New Jersey lose their jobs during the Great Depression.
1993	Christine Todd Whitman is elected New Jersey's first female governor.
1995	The New Jersey Devils win their first Stanley Cup. They win again in 2000 and 2003.
2001	Many New Jersey residents lose their lives in the terrorist attacks on the World Trade Center.

CHAPTER 3

People

More than eight and one-half million people live in New Jersey. Only nine other states have more people.

New Jersey has more people per square mile (sq km) than any other state. Most of the people live close together in cities and towns. Cities such as Newark and Camden are crowded.

Immigrants

More than 17 percent of the people who live in New Jersey were born in another

Hispanics: In the 2000 U.S. Census, 13.3 percent of the people living in New Jersey call themselves Latino or Hispanic. Most of them or their relatives came from Spanish-speaking backgrounds. They may come from different racial backgrounds.

The People of New Jersey

Total Population 8,698,879

White
72.6%

Native Americans and Alaska Native
0.2%

Asian
5.7%

Other
7.9%

Black or African American
13.6%

Percentages are based on 2000 Census.

country. They are called
immigrants. Immigrants
have been coming to the
state for a long time. More
than one hundred years ago,
most immigrants came from
Europe. Some came to find
work, and others came to
find freedom. They all
hoped to have better lives
in their new home. Many
took jobs digging canals,
working in factories, or
laboring on ships.

Millions of people entering the
United States for the first time
landed on Ellis Island. The
island is in both New Jersey
and New York.

Immigrants are still
coming to the state every
day, but they are not coming
just from Europe. They
come from Puerto Rico,
Costa Rica, and Cuba.
They come from China
and India, too. People have
left many countries to make

Famous People of New Jersey

Albert Einstein

Born: March 14, 1879, Ulm, Germany

Died: April 18, 1955, Princeton, New Jersey

Albert Einstein was born in Germany. He became a great **physicist**, and his ideas changed the way people think about time and space. In 1921, he won a Nobel Prize for his work. Later, he moved to New Jersey and worked at the Institute for Advanced Study in Princeton.

new lives for themselves in New Jersey.

These immigrants often come to find jobs. They want their children to learn English and go to school. They bring new ideas to New Jersey. They bring new energy, too.

African Americans

After the Civil War, many black people moved to New Jersey. They wanted to get away from the South and find jobs. Today, about 14 percent of the people in the state are African Americans.

Religion and Education

The people of New Jersey follow many different faiths. Christians are the largest group in the state. Many Jews live there, too. Some Muslims and Hindus also live there.

New Jersey takes learning seriously. The state has had public grade schools since 1817. Its first college opened even earlier.

Queens College was founded in 1766. It is now known as Rutgers, the State University of New Jersey. Princeton University is in New Jersey, too. It is one of the top universities in the nation.

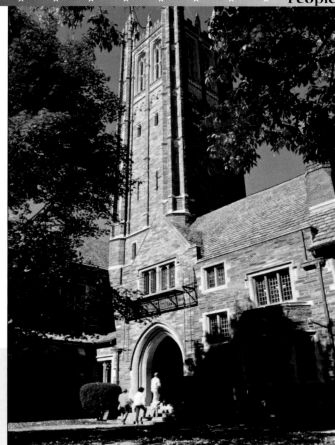

Princeton University is one of the oldest colleges in the United States.

Famous People of New Jersey

Judy Blume

Born: February 12, 1938, Elizabeth, New Jersey

Judy Blume is a famous writer of children's books. Many of her books are set in New Jersey, where she grew up. *Super Fudge* takes place in Princeton. When Judy was young, she did not plan to be a writer. She wanted to be a cowgirl or maybe a spy. When she grew up and had children, she started writing stories. Many children love her books.

The Land

New Jersey is the fourth smallest state. It covers only 7,787 square miles (20,168 sq km). It has water on three sides. The Atlantic Ocean runs along the east and southeast coasts. The Delaware River forms the state border on the west.

The Northern Highlands

Mountains and valleys cover the northern part of New Jersey. The Kitattinny Mountains come first. They form the northwestern border of the state. These mountains are not very tall. Still, they include the state's highest peak, High Point. It is 1,803 feet (550 meters) above sea level.

Oak, maple, and other hardwood trees grow there. Not many big animals live there, but chipmunks, raccoons, and other small creatures are common.

Next to the mountains lies the Appalachian Valley. It has good land for farming. Beyond this big valley are more ridges and valleys. Many of the state's

FUN FACTS

Black Bears

Black bears are the largest animals in New Jersey. They live in forests in the northwest. Many people have moved into this area. Now, the bears sometimes get into their yards and garbage cans. In 2003, New Jersey allowed a bear hunt. People are trying to find better ways to help bears and humans share the land.

NEW JERSEY

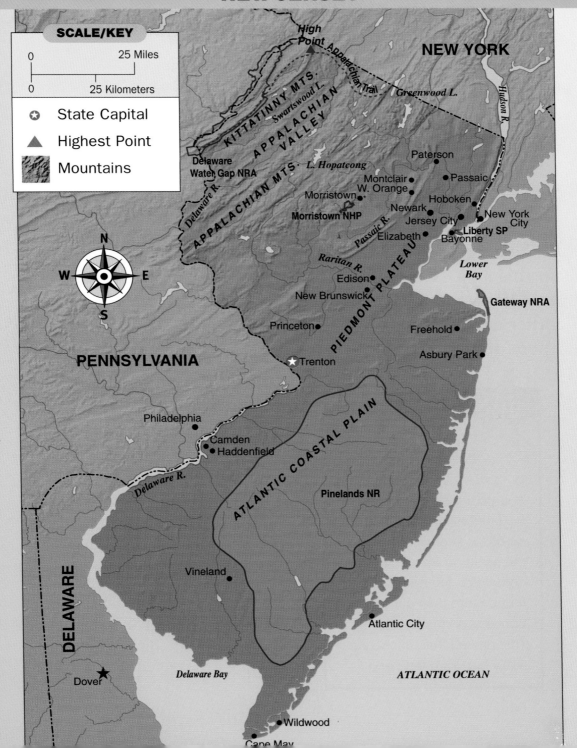

SCALE/KEY

0   25 Miles

0   25 Kilometers

⭐ State Capital

▲ Highest Point

▨ Mountains

NEW YORK

High Point

Swartswood L.

Greenwood L.

KITTATINNY MTS.

APPALACHIAN VALLEY

Appalachian Trail

Hudson R.

APPALACHIAN MTS.

Delaware Water Gap NRA

Delaware R.

L. Hopatcong

Paterson

Montclair
W. Orange

Passaic

Morristown

Hoboken

Morristown NHP

Newark

Jersey City

New York City

Liberty SP

Passaic R.

Elizabeth

Bayonne

Raritan R.

Edison

Lower Bay

New Brunswick

Gateway NRA

Princeton

PIEDMONT PLATEAU

Freehold

Asbury Park

PENNSYLVANIA

⭐ Trenton

Philadelphia

Camden
Haddonfield

ATLANTIC COASTAL PLAIN

Delaware R.

Pinelands NR

DELAWARE

Vineland

Atlantic City

Dover

Delaware Bay

ATLANTIC OCEAN

Wildwood

Cape May

eight hundred lakes and ponds are found there. The largest is Lake Hopatcong. It is 8 miles (13 kilometers) long. The Raritan River runs through this part of the state, too. It is the longest river that is completely within New Jersey.

Deer and coyotes roam in this area. Chipmunks, rabbits, woodchucks, and other small animals live there, too. All of these

Major Rivers
Delaware River
280 miles (451 km) long
Hudson River
306 miles (492 km) long
Passaic River
80 miles (129 km) long

animals are found almost everywhere in New Jersey.

The Piedmont is in the middle of the state. It is a land of rolling hills. All four of the state's biggest cities are located there.

The Southern Plain

South of the Piedmont lies a big, low-lying plain. Known as the Atlantic Coastal Plain, it covers more than half the state. Part of the plain has rich soil for farming. This area gave the state its nickname of the "Garden State." Farther east, salt

FUN FACTS

A Big Find

In 1858, William Foulke dug up a fossil on a farm in Haddonfield. It was a dinosaur **skeleton**, and the skeleton was almost complete. No one had ever found more than a few bones at a time before. This proved that dinosaurs really had lived long ago.

marshes cover many acres, and sandy beaches line the coast. The Pine Barrens is near the coast too. This is an area with poor soil where small bushy pine trees grow.

Protecting the Land

The people of New Jersey want to take care of their beautiful natural places. They have passed laws to control pollution. They do not let people build homes or factories in the Pine Barrens and some of the other wild places.

They also protect the New Jersey coastline. A narrow bar of sand lines the whole coast. Every year, storms wash sand off the beaches. To prevent them from being destroyed, people pile new sand on the beaches every spring. They plant grass on the dunes, too. This helps keep the sand from blowing away or washing into the ocean.

Four Seasons

In New Jersey, summers are hot and humid. Fall brings cool, crisp days and brightly colored leaves. Winters are cold and snowy. Spring brings welcome relief from the cold, along with new leaves and spring flowers.

Great Falls in Paterson, New Jersey, plunges 77 feet (23 meters).

Economy

New Jersey has been an industrial leader for a long time. These days, some call it "the nation's medicine chest" because it makes so many drugs. It also is known for making electronics. **Food processing** is big there, too. The state makes canned vegetables and soups, cookies, candies, pastas, and much more.

Goods from New Jersey are sold all over the world. Ships come and go from

Huge containers are stacked on a ship in Newark, New Jersey. The ship will carry the goods in the containers around the world.

the ports in Newark and Elizabeth. Trucks head north, south, and west on huge highways. Bridges and tunnels connect New Jersey to its neighbors. In this state, **transportation** is big business, too.

Services

Many people in New Jersey work in hospitals, schools, restaurants, and hotels. These people have service jobs. Others service jobs include buying and selling goods to people and companies.

Fewer people work on farms. They raise flowers, tomatoes, cranberries, blueberries, and other crops. Some farms produce milk and eggs. The New Jersey shore yields food products, too. Clams and shellfish come from coastal waters.

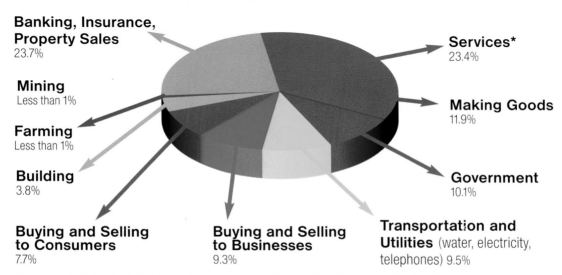

How Money Is Made in New Jersey

Banking, Insurance, Property Sales
23.7%

Mining
Less than 1%

Farming
Less than 1%

Building
3.8%

Buying and Selling to Consumers
7.7%

Buying and Selling to Businesses
9.3%

Transportation and Utilities (water, electricity, telephones) 9.5%

Services*
23.4%

Making Goods
11.9%

Government
10.1%

* Services include jobs in hotels, restaurants, auto repair, medicine, teaching, and entertainment.

Government

The capital of New Jersey is Trenton. This is where the state's leaders work. The state government has three parts, or branches. They are the executive, legislative, and judicial branches.

Executive Branch

The job of the executive branch is to carry out the state's laws. The governor leads this branch. The governor appoints a **cabinet**, or team of people, who help run the executive branch.

The state legislature meets in this New Jersey State Capitol building.

Until recently, the governor was always a man. Then, in 1993, Christine Todd Whitman was elected. She was the first female governor in the state's history.

Woodrow Wilson was elected governor of New Jesey in 1910 and became the twenty-eighth president of the United States in 1913. He led the nation through World War I and then worked for peace.

Legislative Branch

The New Jersey legislature passes new laws and changes old laws. It is made up of two groups. One is the Senate and the other is the General Assembly. They work together.

Judicial Branch

Judges and courts make up the judicial branch. Judges and courts may decide whether people who have been accused of committing crimes are guilty.

Local Government

There are twenty-one counties in New Jersey. Each is run by a group, or board, of citizens. They make sure roads and bridges are kept in good repair.

NEW JERSEY'S STATE GOVERNMENT

Executive		Legislative		Judicial	
Office	**Length of Term**	**Body**	**Length of Term**	**Court**	**Length of Term**
Governor	4 years	Senate (40 members) (1st election of the decade is for 2 years)	2-4 years	Supreme (7 justices)	7 years
		General Assembly (80 members)	2 years	Supreme Court, Appellate Division (32 judges)	7 years

Things to See and Do

I t's easy to have fun in New Jersey! The beach is a good place to start. Crowds flock to the state's sandy beaches every summer. The water is cold, but people still like to swim and ride boogie boards. On Long Beach Island, surfers catch big waves. Children ride roller coasters on the **board-walk** in Wildwood. Nature lovers at Cape May look for migrating hawks and fish for blue crabs.

Sports

This state's sports teams are in the news! The New Jersey Devils

FUN FACTS

Firsts in Sports

New Jersey can claim two important "firsts" in sports. In 1846, Hoboken hosted the first known baseball game between two organized teams. The Knickerbockers played the New York Nine that day. Forty years later, the state had another first. This time it was the first professional basketball game. This game took place in Trenton.

Visitors can beat the heat at a water park in Wildwood, New Jersey.

Lawrence Eugene (Larry) Doby

Born: December 13, 1923, Camden, South Carolina

Died: June 18, 2003, Montclair, New Jersey

Larry Doby played baseball in high school in Paterson. He was a great player. Doby became the first African American to play in the American League. He hit a home run and helped the Cleveland Indians win the World Series in 1948.

hockey team won the Stanley Cup in 1995, 2000, and 2003. The New Jersey Nets played in the National Basketball Association finals in 2002 and 2003. Their games draw big crowds. Football fans watch the New York Jets and New York Giants. They are not New Jersey teams, but they play at the Meadowlands in New Jersey.

Museums

The museums in New Jersey have something for every-one. The New Jersey State Museum is in Trenton. It has natural history displays, ancient bones, and much more. Science is exciting at

The New Jersey Devils brought hockey fame to New Jersey.

the Liberty Science Center in Jersey City. Visitors touch live sea creatures and climb a rock wall. At the Newark Museum Planetarium, they see how the planets and stars light up the night sky. Art is the main draw at places like the Montclair Art Museum.

People of all ages learn about skyscrapers, Hudson River wildlife, energy, and light at the Liberty Science Center in Jersey City.

A living-history museum is a museum that uses actors who pretend to be living in a different time. Waterloo Village is a living-history museum that shows how people lived in colonial days. The Franklin Mineral Museum explores the state's mining history. Kids walk through a life-size mine and dig for minerals. Another interesting museum is on Ellis Island. This island was the first U.S. stop for many

immigrants who were on their way to new lives. The museum tells some of their stories.

Skiing and Fishing

People enjoy all kinds of outdoor activities in New Jersey. Skiers and snow-boarders fly down the slopes at Hidden Valley, one of four ski resorts. The Delaware River is a favorite place for kayaking and rafting. The fishing is good in the lakes, rivers, and ocean beaches. Families pitch tents and hike in New Jersey's state parks.

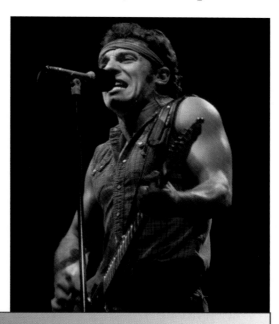

Famous People of New Jersey

Bruce Springsteen

Born: September 23, 1949, Freehold, New Jersey

New Jersey is a great place for music, and one of the state's biggest stars is Bruce Springsteen. This rock 'n' roll legend is from Freehold. When he was young, he sang and played guitar in the beach town of Asbury Park. He and his friends formed the E Street Band. In 1973, he made his first album, "Greetings from Asbury Park, N.J." Some of Springsteen's songs are about New Jersey. His fans call him "The Boss."

★ ★

boardwalk — a wooden walkway that runs along a beach

cabinet — a group of people who work to help a government leader

cargo — goods that are carried on a truck, plane, or ship

colony — a group of people living in a new land but keeping ties with the place they came from

food processing — canning, freezing, or packaging food

Great Depression — a time in the 1930s when many people and businesses lost money

immigrants — people who come to live in one country from another country

industry — a business that produces a product or service

invented — made for the first time

locomotives — engines that provide power to pull trains

physicist — a scientist who studies the laws of matter and energy

race riots — wild, violent acts by crowds usually caused by anger about a difference in treatment of different groups of people

terrorists — people who cause others to fear to achieve their goal

transportation — carrying or moving people or things

Books

The Battlefield Ghost. Margaret Cuyler (Scholastic Books)

The 18 Penny Goose. Sally Walker (Harper Collins)

A Full Hand. Thomas F. Yezerski (Farrar, Straus & Giroux)

A Picture Book of Thomas Alva Edison. David Adler
   (Holiday House)

Rainbow Crow. Nancy Van Laan (Dragonfly Books)

Super Fudge. Judy Blume (Scholastic)

They Called Her Molly Pitcher. Anne Rockwell (Knopf Books
   for Young Readers)

When Washington Crossed the Delaware. Lynn Cheney
   (Simon and Schuster)

Web Sites

The Delaware (Lenape) Tribe of Indians
www.delawaretribeofindians.nsn.us

Edison National Historic Site
www.nps.gov/edis/home.htm

Haddonfield Dinosaur
www.hadrosaurus.com/1858.shtml

New Jersey Legislature's Kids' Page
www.njleg.state.nj.us/kids/index.asp

INDEX

★ ★